The Amish Detective The King Family Arsonist
Hannah Schrock

Table Of Contents

In Heaven

The Englischer Detective

The Service

A Fluttering Heart

Taken

The Secret King

A Second Chance

Epilogue

Be the first to find out about Hannah's Books

A Taster

Gloria sat in the corner of the barn, wiping tears from her eyes as members of the Ordung filed through, one by one, to pay their respects to a beloved family.

It all seemed like a nightmare, one Gloria wished she could awaken from. The last three days had all been part of that nightmare. Everything changed the moment her family received word of the fire. By then, most of their neighbors already knew the story. Life had been spent in a haze since then.

It wasn't just the fact of the fire that worried members of the Ordung, both the communities in which she and her extended family lived. It was the way the fire took place. The police stated it was a clear case of arson, meaning that someone had deliberately started the fire which killed her aunt, uncle and three cousins in their sleep.

Neighbors were in an uproar, and rightly so. How could they protect themselves from this arsonist? Who would be next? There was no question that the act was random—the Kings had no enemies. That simply wasn't the way of the Amish. And they spent very little time outside the community, so there was only limited involvement with the Englischers in town. It wasn't plausible that some person Isaac King knew or did business with would go so far as to set fire to the home. It had to be a sad, troubled person who felt the need to hurt others.

Who would they hurt next?

It was heartbreaking, seeing the pain on the faces of friends and neighbors as they paid their respects. Isaac, a good and hardworking farmer. He had been so well-loved. Esther, always ready with a helping hand and a gentle smile. The two of them had been a strong couple, their commitment to one another second only to their commitment to Gott. There they were. Like second parents to Gloria for as long as she could remember. Both of them in their simple wooden caskets.

Then there were the other three caskets, and Gloria's heart broke a little further when she picked her cousin Susan's out from the three. Susan who was more like a sister to Gloria than a cousin. Whose loyalty and devotion never wavered. Gloria had always wanted to be more like Susan, who was endlessly patient and good to everyone she knew. She had never so much as told a lie, and now she was gone.

And the smaller caskets. Jacob and Elijah, the twins. Only ten years old. They would never grow up to be good men like their father. It seemed as though tears would never stop flowing from Gloria's eyes.

It was worse for her mother, Uncle Isaac's younger sister. She was inconsolable—throughout the days following the fire, Gloria had woken in the middle of the night to the sound of her mother's tears. It seemed as though they might never end.

It was true that faith in Gott that helped the Amish through difficult times, but this was far beyond anything anyone had ever encountered. Not just grief, which everyone must face at one time or another, but fear of the unknown. An Amish person's life generally fell into a distinct, routine pattern. This terrible tragedy had destroyed that pattern.

Even from her quiet corner seat, Gloria overheard the grumblings of several of the community's most respected leaders. They were considering holding a meeting to form teams of men to keep watch on the homes and farms of their neighbors. Never had anything like this been considered in the past. Gloria felt somehow as though so much of what she loved about her life was slipping away. The peace, tranquility, trust. It was the same for all the others. Would they even have a decent night's sleep while waiting to see whose home was next?

"Gloria, are you well?" One of the neighbors, Mrs. Stolztfus, approached.

"As well as can be, thank you," she replied. Her heart wasn't in her words. She felt cold inside.

"Your Mamm seems to be holding up well, all things considered."

"Yes, all things considered." It wasn't in Gloria's nature to be short or sharp, especially with one of her elders, but the older woman couldn't seem to get the message that she didn't wish to speak. It was all too strenuous. Even basic conversation was too much.

"You and your cousin Susan were very close, I know. I remember when you were just little girls, running barefoot along the outside of your home."

Gloria clenched her fist to keep from crying out loud. Didn't Mrs. Stoltzfus understand she was causing pain? Maybe, one day, it would be possible to sit and think of Susan and smile. Maybe Gloria would be able to reminisce about the times she spent with her sweet cousin and remember them fondly, instead of wishing them back with all her might. If only she could go back.

Mrs. Stoltzfus clicked her tongue in sympathy. "To think of something like this happening to Isaac King, of all people. Only the most pious person anyone had ever known, and the friendliest. If it could happen to him, it could happen to any of us."

Gloria had heard it all before, whispered and murmured from one neighbor to another. She gave the same response she had for days. "We must trust in Gott."

"Of course, of course. I only wish the person responsible were caught for what they did. I'm sure it would be easier for your poor Mamm to get over the loss of her brother if she knew the person who took his life was behind bars, where he could hurt no one else."

Then, she walked away, and Gloria couldn't help but breathe a sigh of relief. She had felt suffocated by the older woman's presence. The air felt clearer, cooler.

Why did people feel the need to cloak their curiosity and own selfish need to fret and worry under the mask of care? Gloria knew her neighbor was only venting her fear, and maybe even relishing the excitement of the situation—morbid though that was. Why couldn't people behave that way amongst themselves and leave those who mourned alone with their grief?

Susan's casket. Gloria's eyes kept falling on it. She remembered the gold of Susan's hair, and the cornflower blue of her eyes. Those eyes that had laughed and sparkled, always full of joy. Gloria would never know another person like her. My life will always be a little darker, she thought.

She thought about what Mrs. Stoltzfus said, too, about Uncle Isaac's piousness and how respected and trusted he had been. It was all true, all of it, and it added just another layer to the shock and horror of the event.

If only I had visited Susan when I said I would. It was something she'd berate herself over for the rest of her life. She was sure of it. If only she hadn't been so busy getting her next quilt ready for sale, she could have spent time with her cousin before…before the fire.

I'll never make a mistake like that again. She would never pass up the opportunity to spend time with her loved ones. Nothing was more important than that. There was no guarantee that any of them would be around tomorrow. If there was nothing else to be taken from the tragedy, Gloria thought, that was lesson enough.

Her father, brothers and sisters all gathered together toward the front of the crowd, near where the caskets sat. She wondered if anyone thought it strange that she sat alone—there was no missing the eyes that had watched her throughout the day. People asking themselves why she sat alone. If they had bothered to ask, she would have told them it was too painful to be near the caskets, even if it meant being near her family. She had to be alone with her thoughts, her grief.

She smoothed a long strand of auburn hair back beneath her kapp. She'd been a little lax with her grooming that day, her mind a million miles away.

Just like Susan was. A million miles away, in Heaven. Of course she was in Heaven. That was the only place a person like her could go.

Gloria wiped another tear, one of many endlessly streaming down her face.

There was a bit of a commotion at the barn doors. Gloria turned to see who had entered, and was surprised to see an Englischer. His tan suit, brown shoes and sunglasses set him apart right away. So did his lack of facial hair, as all men his age in the Amish faith grew beards after baptism.

He looked around the room, removing the glasses in order to see better. In the light from the oil lamps hanging from the rafters, Gloria finally recognized him. He was some sort of a policeman. She had seen him over the last three days, here and there. Normally hanging around on the edges of crowds, looking and listening. It was unnerving, feeling as though she and her people were being observed like that. Unnerving but not unusual, since being watched by Englischers was a fact of life for the Amish. Whenever Gloria went to town to sell her quilts, there was never any shortage of Englischers watching and pointing, whispering behind their hands. They'd even pulled up to her family's home on many occasions in their cars. As though the Amish existed as a form of entertainment.

This man at least seemed respectful. He kept his distance from the group of mourners. He was only going his job, Gloria reminded herself. He wasn't watching out of curiosity. She did wish he would have picked a better time to visit, though.

She couldn't take her eyes from him, even though she knew she should. He was fascinating. And handsome. This was the first chance she'd had to observe him, instead of the other way around. His dark brown hair, the bit of shadow on his cheeks. He looked tired—Gloria thought he must have been spending endless hours on the case, and her heart went out to him. He was trying to find the person responsible for the tragedy which befell her family. It meant more than he knew, she was sure.

He caught the eye of her Daed, who touched his wife's arm to get her attention. She turned and, when she saw the officer, rose from her chair. Gloria stood immediately. It was one thing for a stranger, policeman or no, to be there. It was another for him to bother her mother in her time of grief.

By the time she reached them, he was already asking questions. She heard him say something about additional family members, but her mother shook her head. When she reached them, Gloria placed a concerned hand on her mother's shoulder and turned to face the officer.

His eyes fell on her. "Excuse me, miss, but I have some questions for your mother which I think would be best asked solely of her."

So he knew who she was already. He'd already been asking questions, evidently.

"I'm sure you do, and I would like to hear them for myself." She turned to her mother. "Is that all right?"

"If the detective does not mind."

Gloria turned to the detective and waited with an expectant smile. He must have known there was no way for him to dissuade her, though it was obvious from the way he cleared his throat before speaking that he wasn't over-fond of speaking in front of her.

"Actually, I don't have anything else to ask. I wanted to assure you that we're doing everything in our power to find the culprit behind the crime." He smiled at Gloria. "We've never actually met. I'm Detective Paul Miller."

"Gloria Kauffman," she replied, smiling slightly.

"I'm very sorry for your loss, Miss Kauffman." He smiled at her Mamm and shook her hand. The smile changed his face—he was normally so serious, stern. When he smiled he looked younger. "I'll leave you, now. I'm sorry to have disrupted the wake."

"Would you like to stay for refreshments?" Gloria smiled fondly at her Mamm, who was cordial and kind even in the worst of times.

"No, thank you, ma'am. I'm sure you would rather proceed without the reminder of the police hanging around. Thank you for the offer." He nodded at the two of them and left the barn.

Gloria couldn't stand to see him go without finding out more. She ran after him, not caring who saw. Finding out about the arson was more important.

"Excuse me," she murmured when she caught up to him. She touched him arm purely out of reflex, then pulled her hand back as though he burned to the touch.

He turned back to her. "Yes, Miss Kauffman?"

"Detective, is there any new information about the murderer? Anything at all?"

He frowned. "Miss Kauffman, it's very unusual for a detective to discuss a case with the family of the victim before there's any sure suspect. I can't share speculation with you."

Her frown mirrored his. "But you do know something?"

"I can't tell you either way. I'm sorry, I'm sure it's frustrating. We're just as frustrated at the station, believe me." He turned away as if to go, and she touched his arm again. Again, she felt it was improper, but she was desperate.

"Miss Kauffman, it would be best if you go back in with your family. You need each other at a time like this. Let us do our job, and we'll let you know if there's any further news. You'll be the first to know, in fact." Again, he turned away.

Gloria went around him, standing in his way. He sighed in exasperation.

"I want to help you."

His eyes went wide. They were a deep blue, the color of the sky at twilight. "You what?"

"I want to help. I'm sure there's something I can tell you that you don't already know."

"You mean there are secrets we aren't aware of?"

She blushed and took a step back. "No. I didn't mean it that way."

"How did you mean it, then?"

"I only meant to say that I'm close with the family. Susan was like my sister. We Amish—we're close, anyway. We live our lives together, helping one another. We depend on each other. I'm sure you don't know that."

"I'm sure I don't," he said, with a wry smile.

"So you see, we know a lot about each other. Add to that my closeness with my cousin and, well, you see what I mean. I'm sure I can offer something of value to the investigation."

He looked skeptical, his eyes narrowing. "I'm not sure. We already know a lot about the family. We've spoken to the neighbors, for miles in all directions."

"I grew up with them. I'm sure there's something you've missed. I only want the chance to help."

She felt his eyes on her as he sized her up, and drew herself up to her full height. She was small, especially when compared to his tall height, but she was stronger than she looked. The detective would find that out, if he ever gave her a chance.

"You won't leave me alone until I agree to talk with you, will you?" His face wore a wry smile. He had a dry sense of humor, Gloria noticed.

She had to smile, too. "No, I won't. You'll be saving yourself a lot of time if you just let me have my say. I know you won't regret it."

He shrugged. "All right. What if we meet at the coffee shop tomorrow afternoon?"

The smile faded from her face. "The funeral is tomorrow afternoon."

"Oh. That was clumsy of me."

Gloria swallowed over the lump in her throat. "That's all right. You didn't mean it."

"I plan to be at the funeral as well—standing off to the back, of course. I wouldn't want to get in the way."

This surprised her so much, she forgot the threat of tears. "Why would you do that?"

"It's something we do—the police, I mean. I want to be there to keep an eye out for any suspicious looking people."

"But only the Amish will be there. People like me. You don't think it was someone from the community, do you?"

He winced. "No. And I think that should be as much as we discuss about it. I'll meet up with you after the services are finished."

Gloria's eyes cut toward the barn. She wondered how her family would feel about her running off to meet with an Englischer, detective or not. It was all in the name of getting answers, though.

"All right. I'll look for you."

"I don't think it'll be too tough to find me." He grinned, and Gloria giggled before she could help herself. Yes, he would stand out in his fine suit, so unlike the plain clothes of her people.

She hurried back to the barn, then, fearful of being discovered with the Englischer. Giggling when everyone else was in mourning. The talk would never end.

On the day of the funeral after a religious service was held in the home, the long line of buggies proceeded to the cemetery. The service, held the following day in a small plot of land designated for people of their community, was the most difficult thing of all.

Gloria wasn't sure she could bear up under the grief at times. Listening to her Mamm's strangled sobs, which she tried so hard to stifle. Seeing the five simple wooden caskets lined up in a row. That was the worst. The finality of it. Gloria had never lost anyone close to her before.

She busied herself with the task of keeping her younger siblings together and making sure they were all right. She was the oldest, at twenty-three, and her youngest brother was only eight. Eli didn't understand very much about what had happened, as he was too young to be exposed to exactly how so many members of his family died at once. It was a distraction, at least, to check on him from time to time, along with her other two brothers and two sisters. None of them were as close to their cousins as Gloria was to Susan, though little Jacob had often played with his twin cousins, as they were the same age.

So many people attended the service, it was almost beyond reason. Yet Isaac had that sort of effect on people throughout his entire life. He was a good man, the sort who drew others to him without trying. His wisdom and faith in Gott were well-known throughout the Ordung, as was his generosity. Gloria saw many pairs of red-rimmed eyes in the crowd.

She couldn't help searching for the detective on the edges of the crowd. He'd been in her mind ever since their meeting the day before. She'd been unable to focus on her chores or much of anything else. It was a welcome distraction, really, after the depth of grief she'd suffered for days before that.

Then, she saw him. He did stand out, in a light-colored pair of pants and striped shirt. Nothing so bold would ever be worn by a member of her community. He wore his sunglasses, so Gloria couldn't tell where he looked…or who he looked at.

Her eyes scanned the crowd of mourners. Was it possible that Detective Miller had her questioning the people she'd lived alongside for her entire life? It couldn't be one of them. It had to be an outsider.

Still…wasn't Mr. Lapp acting rather furtively? He kept looking up at the others from beneath lowered brows. Why was he so uneasy?

What about Mr. Yoder? He was probably the only person in the community to ever have a quarrel with Uncle Isaac. Was it one of them? Did they have it in them to commit such a terrible crime?

It was unthinkable. Aside from the plain, black-clothed mourners there was not a single Englischer in sight. It looked as though the detective's hunch was wrong.

It didn't matter. The hunch was enough to get the detective to attend services, which made it easier to meet with him afterward. The only question was how Gloria could get away without her parents knowing of the meeting.

It turned out to be a non-issue. By the time the mourners departed, there were so many grouped around her parents that Gloria slipped away easily, after telling her sister Martha that she was going to speak with one of Susan's friends and would be home later. As soon as she was out of her sister's field of vision, however, she made a beeline for Detective Miller.

"That was a very moving service," he said. "Again, I'm sorry for your loss."

"Thank you." She looked back over the crowd, a lump in her throat. It had never been more clear that she would never see any of the King family again.

"Shall we?" he asked.

"Certainly, Detective." They began to make the short walk to the local coffee shop.

"You can call me Paul, you know. We don't have to be so formal."

Gloria flushed, and she shook her head. "I don't know that it would be right for me to do that."

"Why?"

"It's a little too familiar, wouldn't you say?"

"Would you say it?"

She bit her lip and looked away, to hide her smile. "Well," she murmured once she was able to speak without giggling, "maybe it's not so bad. It's easier than calling you 'Detective' all the time."

"I agree. So Paul it is."

"All right…Paul. And you can call me Gloria." She glanced at him from the corner of her eye as they walked.

"Thank you, Gloria." They reached the coffee house, and Paul held the door for her. She was glad for the air conditioning when they stepped inside—it was one of the few luxuries forbidden to those in her faith that she genuinely wished she could have the chance to enjoy on unseasonably warm days like the present one.

"Can I order something for you? You look a little piqued."

"I'll order for myself, thank you." Referring to him by his first name was one thing, but allowing him to buy her a cup of kaffe was another.

She ordered a simple iced kaffe with plenty of milk and sugar. Paul offered to wait for it while Gloria found a table, so she had a seat near the window. It was a small relief to sit and relax on such a trying day. While she waited for Paul to join her, she took the opportunity to watch him. He had a lean, athletic body and a sort of casual confidence which was disarming. He was even more handsome than she remembered him being, and it had been less than a day since they last spoke. How could she have forgotten the very deep blue of his eyes, which she saw when he smiled at her from the counter? His sunglasses did him no justice.

It was then that Gloria shook herself. She was thinking far too much about him, and it wasn't right. He was very nice, and helpful, and interesting. But that was where it stopped. Getting too close to Englischers only led to trouble, as there was no way for the two worlds to mix. Besides, her head was too clogged with thoughts of her family to worry about a handsome man.

He sat across from her, handing her the tall cup full of milky coffee. The first sip was refreshing, and bolstered Gloria's confidence.

"What is it you wanted to talk with me about?" Paul asked, sipping his own frothy concoction.

"Susan was a good girl," she said, wanting to be sure Paul understood. "My family were good people."

"I wouldn't imagine them as anything else," he replied. "I've heard nothing but good things about them."

She nodded. "What you've heard is true. They were all good

people. Which was why it was so surprising when a young man accosted us."

"Accosted you? When was this?" He pulled out a notepad and began scribbling.

"It happened several times. Over the course of at least two, maybe three years."

"And you didn't tell anyone?" Paul's face showed plain surprise.

"We didn't think much of it—honestly, we didn't. At first, we thought he was only a customer at the farmer's market. That's where we would sell our family's produce. I would also sell quilts at the souvenir shop next to the market."

"But you say he accosted you."

"At first, he walked close to us. Very close. It was clear he followed us. He didn't even try to be sneaky about it." She shuddered lightly, remembering how it had felt to be followed by him. There was a strange sort of look about him.

"How far did he follow you? For how long, I mean?"

She shrugged. "Maybe halfway home. It was hard to tell. One minute he would be there, the next he wouldn't. We told ourselves it was coincidence. That he lived nearby—some farms in our area aren't owned by Amish families. Or that he frequented the market, or the shop. Many people do."

Paul nodded. "Around how many times would you say that happened?"

She thought about it. "Maybe ten times, or a dozen. But over three years, that hardly seems like anything to worry about. And he never got very close, and never attempted to speak to us. You see why we didn't mention it to anyone." It seemed important to defend herself, as though she had missed something very important. Something that might have saved her cousin's life.

"Yes, I see." Paul made a note. "Did he ever approach you?"

She frowned, remembering that last encounter all too well. "Yes. The last time we saw him, he did."

"When was that?"

"Three weeks ago. It's still very clear to me."

"Good. Tell me about it, please."

She stared off into space, bringing up the images in her head. "We stopped by the souvenir shop to pick up the money from the latest quilt sales. It was getting late, after six o'clock, and many people were leaving for the day so it was a little hectic."

She closed her eyes, and she was back in the shop. She had just folded up a wad of bills and put it in her small purse when Susan noticed the young man.

"He stood only six feet away from us, at most. Susan saw him while I was counting the money. She turned away from him, toward me, and took my arm. She whispered that he stood just behind her. I looked right at him before I could stop myself. I felt a chill go through me. It sounds funny, but I did. His eyes were so dark and angry."

"Did he say anything?"

"Not at first. I looked away and told Susan to ignore him. We left the shop and started walking home."

"You didn't ask for help?"

She looked at him, feeling helpless. "That's not what we do. We don't usually ask outsiders for help. You have to understand."

"I do. Believe me." He made a note. "So you walked home."

"Yes. Or we started to, anyway. I was so scared, my knees shook. There was something different about him this time. Normally, he seemed strange but standoffish. This time he seemed desperate, like he was determined to follow us home. We nearly ran, we walked so fast." She trailed off, her heart racing just as it had that night. She had been terrified, even to the point of considering flagging down a passing car.

"Finally, he caught up with us." She stared at the table, whispering now. It was all too much to bear.

"Why don't you take a sip of your drink? Or I could get you some water. Why don't I do that?" Paul got up without waiting for her to reply and asked the girl behind the counter for water. Gloria was too overwhelmed to thank him. It took her a long time to speak again after taking the first drink.

"When he caught us," she continued, "he grabbed Susan by the arm." She took her own arm in her hand to show him, holding her bicep in a tight grip. "And he pulled her to him, hard. She cried out. So did I. I screamed, actually."

"Of course, you did. Did he say anything to her?"

"He screamed in her face. He said, 'Sister, I just want to talk', and he shook her."

"He said that? He called her 'sister'?"

"Yes, just like that." Paul's brow furrowed, and he made a note.

"What did you do then?"

"We ran. I took Susan's other arm and pulled, and he let go, and we ran as fast as we could. All the way back to her family's farm. We told Uncle Isaac all about it, while Aunt Esther made up dinner for us."

"Were you upset?"

"Terribly. Susan was shaking, and crying, and rubbing her arm where he'd held her. She had bruises and everything. He was very rough, and he screamed so loudly. It was so scary."

Paul frowned, shaking his head. "What did your uncle say?"

Gloria took another sip of her water and sighed. "That was the strangest part of all. He totally dismissed us."

"He what?" Paul's eyes widened. "Did you tell him all of it? Every last bit?"

"Every last bit. He acted like it didn't mean anything."

Paul shook his head and made another note.

"In fact," Gloria added, thinking it over, "he even told us that we were exaggerating. He wasn't there. How would he know? But that was what he said. He told us the boy was just looking for the time."

"I don't mind telling you, Gloria, but that seems strange. Very strange."

"I thought it was, too."

"What did Susan think? Did she tell you?"

"Yes, she told me. She was ready to forget the entire thing ever happened. And she did."

"Did you?"

Gloria smiled slightly. "What do you think? Clearly not, if I remember it so well."

He smiled, too. "So you felt it was important to tell me about this.

Does that mean you think the young man had something to do with the fire?"

"Jah. I do."

"You seem very certain," Paul said, tapping a pen against his notepad. From what Gloria could see of it, upside down as it was to her eyes, his writing was chicken scratch. She smiled to herself.

"I am," she said. "There's no one else. The family had no enemies, and this is not something our people do. It's just not. It had to be the outsider. He followed us, he laid hands on Susan, he yelled at her. He seemed very unstable. It was terrible."

"Do you think he was obsessed with Susan?"

"I don't know. It makes sense, doesn't it? Why else would he have followed her? He might have followed us from a distance that night, or some other time when we didn't notice him. It wouldn't have taken much to find out where Susan lived."

"You think he was obsessed enough to light her house on fire?" He wasn't mocking her, she knew. His voice was gentle, tender. She heard concern in it, and was touched by it.

"There's just as much a chance of it being him as anyone else." She was firm, certain. She'd been thinking about it for days, ever since word came to the family of the fire. "As soon as I heard of the fire, after the shock wore off, I thought of him. His was the first face that came to mind. Only his."

"You remember his face, then?"

"Very clearly."

"Do you think you could speak with a sketch artist?"

She frowned. "What does that mean?"

He grinned and looked off to the side. "I keep forgetting you don't know these things."

"Oh? Does my clothing not remind you?"

He laughed outright. "I don't see your clothing. I just see a girl. A very nice girl."

She blushed, and it was her turn to look away. "You didn't answer my question."

"Oh, of course." He cleared his throat. "It's an artist who creates drawings of suspects based on descriptions. They ask questions and then draw what's described to them. You'd be surprised how talented they are—I've seen sketches which look startlingly like the person in question. Especially when the one giving the description remembers the suspect very well."

"I see. I do remember him well."

"What does he look like?" The pen was in his hand again, poised over the paper.

"He's tall—not as tall as you."

"You noticed how tall I am?" He didn't look up, but there was a smile in his voice.

"It would be impossible not to, since you're so much taller than I am." Again, she blushed furiously, and was glad his eyes were trained on the paper. "Aside from that, he had blonde hair, cut short. Dark eyes. A little, what do you call it?" She rubbed her fingers along her chin, around the sides of her mouth.

"Goatee."

Gloria nodded. "Yes. One of those, very well trimmed. He has a stocky build, a little thick. Not heavy, but not thin."

"I see what you mean. How old would you say he was?"

"Around my age."

"Which is?" he smiled.

"Twenty-three."

"A baby." He smirked as he jotted the note.

"Do you think I should talk to the sketch artist, still?"

He nodded grimly. "They'll ask more specific questions and will be able to make a much clearer picture. You'll be able to tell them what should change—the nose a little thinner, the jaw more square or round."

She bit her lip and looked out the window. So many people out there. None of them knew the pain she was in. None of them knew that she felt as though she was drowning in grief, and confusion.

"Is that a problem?" Paul asked.

She shook her head, still looking away. "I'm worried about my family finding out that I'm getting involved."

"Why is that? They don't approve?"

She turned back to him, and his eyes were so kind. There couldn't be anything wrong with confiding in him. "They don't want me meddling."

"Meddling? You have real information. You should see some of the people I deal with all the time. They call at all hours, they show up at the station. They want to play armchair detective." He laughed at her look of confusion. "Amateur detectives, from the comfort of their living room armchair."

She smiled and nodded. "I see."

"You, on the other hand? You have something real to tell me. Something that could help us catch the person responsible. I would think that would be the most important thing of all. Then again…" He smiled sadly. "I know how exclusive the Amish can be."

She bristled at his words. "Oh, really? You know so much about my people?"

"Easy, easy," he said, holding his hands up. "I'm your friend here, not your enemy."

She softened. "I'm sorry. It's just that there are so many who think they understand us, but they don't. They looked at us like some oddity." She glanced toward the people in line, who stared at her with unabashed fascination. She looked at Paul and nodded her head ever so slightly in their direction. "See what I mean?"

He didn't have to look. "I know what you mean. I do. You have no idea how much."

"Anyway, my family was very careful not to give me many details about the crime. Honestly, I got more information from hearsay than from them. If it wasn't so heinous, and the rest of the community wasn't so scared, they wouldn't talk to you at all. We like to settle things among ourselves."

He tilted his head to the side. "I wonder how you haven't figured it out yet."

"Figured what out?"

"That I used to be Amish, too."

Gloria thought her eyes might fall out of her head, they went so wide. Her mouth hung open. "You?"

He laughed at her surprise. "Yes, me. For most of my life."

She stuttered. "Wh—where did you live? H—how old were you?"

"I'm originally from Indiana. A very strict community. We didn't even have a gas refrigerator, like so many others do now. When I went on Rumspringa, I decided it was best for me to leave the Ordung and live among the Englisch."

She shook her head, her mouth still slightly open. "I don't believe it. You look just like one of them."

He chuckled. "I am one of them, Gloria. I've lived this life for almost ten years. I went to college and joined the police force right after. I'm the youngest detective in the squad. I was assigned to this case because of my past."

"Oh, I see." It all made sense. "They thought because you know about us, you would be best to investigate."

"Exactly. So, here I am." He shrugged.

"What about your family?"

He swallowed hard and looked out the window at the growing darkness. It was early autumn, the days growing shorter all the time. The sky outside was turning a deep blue that matched his eyes, Gloria thought.

"They took it hard," he finally said. "Very hard. Mamm cried for days. She cried so hard that at one point, I considered changing my mind just so she wouldn't hurt anymore. It hurt me, knowing how much I'd hurt her. Daed, on the other hand, refused to speak to me. He wouldn't acknowledge my presence in the world. Literally."

"I'm very sorry," she whispered. It was unimaginable to her, living separately from her family. She loved them so much, and depended on them as part of her life. She adored her parents and her brothers and sisters, even if the latter could be a bit much at times. Leaving them would be like cutting part of herself off. She saw the pain in his face, heard it in his voice. It wasn't easy for him. He must have been very committed to his decision.

"I think Gott has forgiven me," he said. "I believe He understands. I do everything I can to help people. I solve cases and take criminals off the street. I try to make it up to Him every day."

Gloria sighed. He sounded so pained.

"You see what I mean, though, when I tell you that I understand the exclusivity of the Amish. I know how closed-off they are. Everything is settled among themselves, as you said. It hasn't been easy to get information out of people. Only when they remember how easily it could have been their house, their family, do they open up. Even then, they sound resentful. Like they'd rather tell me to get lost than tell me anything that would help the investigation. It's frustrating, to say the least."

"I can't imagine. Or maybe I can, since every time I bring it up they act like I'm crazy for wanting to talk about it. Like I should forget or something."

He nodded. "Well, you can't forget, and I don't expect you to. If you ever want to talk, you can…oh. You can't call me." He laughed at himself. "I still forget sometimes."

"We have a phone booth, down the road."

"There you go. You can call me from the phone booth." He handed her a business card with his name and phone number. "If you think of something, or need to talk, you can call me and I'll come get you."

For a split second, it all seemed so nice. Yes, she could do that. She could call him and they could go somewhere and she could talk about the things that were on her mind, and he would understand and make her laugh, and she would feel better.

She should have known he was originally Amish. It would explain the connection she felt with him when they first met.

Then she reminded herself that it could never be. She was walking a thin line with the detective, one which required great care. She couldn't become too attached to him. She already had.

"I should go home." She stood suddenly, nearly knocking the table on its side.

Paul looked surprised. "Oh. All right." He stood as well. "Let me drive you home."

She blushed deeply. "I don't think that would be a good idea."

"You know you can trust me, right?"

I don't think I can trust myself. "I don't think my family would be happy to see me in a car with a detective. They don't even know I'm with you right now."

"Oh, sneaking out, huh?" He chuckled, but stopped when he saw the horrified look on her face.

"I felt it was important," she defended herself.

"It was. And I get the feeling that you have a very strong sense of right and wrong. Don't lose that, Gloria Kauffman."

Her heart fluttered, and her stomach turned an excited flip-flop. Her palms went clammy. It was all so delicious and intoxicating, and so dangerous. She shook herself to clear her head.

"Thank you for taking the time to meet with me," she said.

"I can meet you here again, tomorrow. So you can meet with the sketch artist, I mean. I can take you there."

She took a deep, shaky breath. "All right. I can meet you after my morning chores. How about eight o'clock?"

He blew out a sharp breath, then shook his head. "One thing I don't miss is the early mornings. How about nine, instead? That way the artist will be available."

She agreed, and they walked outside together. It was a little thrilling, knowing she would meet him the next day. And it was completely proper. There was nothing wrong with it. She was doing what she felt was right.

"Are you absolutely sure I can't at least drive you part way? I know how important it is for you to not use cars, but this is your safety we're talking about here." He looked so sincere, so earnest, it touched her heart.

Still, it didn't make it right. "I don't think so. Thank you, though. I'll see you here tomorrow at nine o'clock."

He sighed once it was clear that he couldn't get through to her. "I look forward to it," he said, smiling softly. What was it about him that made her heart flutter so?

Gloria turned away, glad for the deepening darkness that would cover up the flush in her cheeks. She was breathless, almost giddy.

It was good for her to walk home not just because she needed to avoid being discovered, but because she needed time to calm down. If she walked into the house with flushed cheeks and a nervous giggle, it would give her away in a heartbeat.

What was she supposed to do with herself? No matter how many times she reminded herself of the way she was taught, of all the reasons it was wrong for her to become involved with an Englischer—even emotionally, even without his knowledge—she was lost in a spiral of excitement and confusion and the thrill of something new.

She reminded herself that Gott was the most important part of her life. Not even her devotion to her family and community. It was Gott, first and foremost, and every step she took toward disobeying His commands and the Amish laws was a step away from Him. It wasn't always easy to remember that in the moment, when her heart pounded and her blood rushed and she felt tingly all over. When her hands shook and went a little clammy, and she felt flushed and breathless. Gott seemed like a faraway concept in that moment.

All the more reason for her to avoid spending more time with him.

It was a heartbreaking thought, but that didn't make it any less true. She could tell herself all she wanted that she was only helping with the investigation, but that wasn't strictly all there was to it. If nothing else, Gloria had always been an honest person—that day was the first in which she'd told a lie to her family, and her conscience still stung. If she got further involved with Paul, there was no telling how much worse things could get. She'd be led down the road of temptation again and again, and the temptations would get bigger every time.

When she thought about never seeing him again, though, her heart ached. Not as much as it had since the fire, but more than she thought was possible over a person she'd only just met.

***

She made it home in one piece, and by the time she got there she was resigned to the idea of never seeing Paul again. It was wrong.

Her parents were still too grief-stricken to pay much attention to her arrival. They were happy to accept the excuse that she'd been visiting with Susan's friends—they knew how hard Gloria took the loss of her best friend. She felt guilty, soul-crushingly guilty, but couldn't bring herself to tell the truth. It was easier for them to believe she'd been with friends than with the police.

The mood in the house was somber, quieter than usual. It was always quiet, of course, but this was a different kind of quiet. Normally, there was peace and tranquility at home. This quiet was filled with sadness. She'd never known the difference before, because that level of sadness had never touched her life.

Mamm asked if she'd eaten, and fixed a plate of food. They'd just said goodnight to their last visitor before Gloria arrived, she said. Her eyes were ringed with dark circles, a result of all the crying she'd been doing.

"Mamm, please, sit down. Rest. Take it easy on yourself." Gloria helped her mother into a chair and kissed her forehead. She wished there was a way to remove some of the intense grief from their lives.

There was. She sat down to her supper and thought it over. As long as she could remind herself against becoming too attached to Paul, there was no reason why she couldn't speak with the sketch artist. Knowing who killed the King family wouldn't bring them back, but it would surely bring some measure of peace. It had to. Something had to.

That was why Gloria left home the next morning, under the pretence of checking to see how her quilts were faring at the souvenir shop. She kept a close eye on the time all morning, making sure to have her chores done by eight-thirty. Plenty of time to be at the coffee shop by nine.

Before leaving, Gloria made sure her hair was neatly arranged, her kapp pinned securely in place. She tried to ignore the flush of color in her cheeks. It wasn't excitement over seeing Paul, she told herself. It was excitement over helping catch the arsonist. That was what made her heart race as she walked out the front door.

The main road was still mostly empty, the businesses in town not opening for another half-hour. The tourists didn't often show up until late morning at the earliest, especially during the week. If it had been a Saturday, there would have been dozens of cars to avoid as she walked along the side of the wide main road.

There was only one car, and it was parked only a quarter mile down the road from where her family's property ended. As she approached, she thought nothing of it—cars broke down all the time. Only this car was running. When she drew near, one of the doors swung open.

Horror spread through her before she could think. Her heart nearly stopped, and she froze in place like a frightened animal. It was him. And he was just as she remembered him.

Especially his eyes. His dark, angry eyes.

Before she could turn and run, he caught up to her and grabbed her by the arm, then put his other hand over her mouth. Though she kicked and screamed, he was too strong for her, and within seconds he threw her into the back of the car, closed the door and sped off.

She screamed again and again, pulling at the door handles. He had them locked somehow, and she couldn't unlock them. She wouldn't even know how, and her fingers fumbled around.

"Please! Let me go!" She pounded on the windows, tried to get the attention of passerby. There were so few of them, though. It didn't help that he took narrow backroads.

No matter how loudly Gloria screamed or how hard she pounded on the windows, the man acted as though she wasn't there. He ignored her completely. He mumbled to himself instead of acknowledging her. She couldn't make out anything he said, only that he was very passionate about it. His voice rose and fell, words tumbling out. He even snarled more than once.

Eventually, she ran out of strength and sat perfectly still. Once the initial flurry of excitement and fear passed, she was left frozen again, as she had been on the side of the road. Why hadn't she fled sooner? She might have been able to outrun him.

A large, abandoned barn came into view. They were far outside town at this point—so far, there was no way she could possibly run away. She didn't even know where they were. All Gloria could do was wait for him to get on with whatever he had planned.

He stopped the car, then came around to get her.

This was it.

"Get out." He pulled her roughly by the arm, and she let out a whimper without meaning to. She had the feeling the less noise she made, the better. It was one thing to try to escape on the road, but now he wasn't driving. He could focus solely on her.

The barn was as abandoned as she'd thought it was when they drove up, filled with reminders of the previous owners and their tools. She wondered dimly where they were, and if they knew what would happen in their barn after they left it. Did they know she would be killed there? Because there was no doubting what he had in mind, not when he dragged her as hard as he did and expressed no reaction to her frantic cries.

He still mumbled, ceaselessly, and with the same anger he'd shown in the car. He was deeply disturbed—obviously. It chilled Gloria's blood to hear him. He wouldn't look at her, which somehow was even more upsetting than when he turned to her with his cold, flat eyes.

There was a chair near the door. He shoved her into it, not caring whether or not he hurt her. She banged her tailbone, hard, against the wood. Her cry of pain went unheard, or might as well have judging from the lack of reaction from her captor.

There was a length of rope on the floor. It looked new. Gloria realized in horror that he'd planned it out in advance. He knew he was going to take her there, he knew he had to restrain her. How long had he been putting it together? How long had he been following her without her knowing about it? He knew about her appointment at the coffee shop, which was why he waited for her. She shivered.

Where is Gott? Gloria wondered, as her captor tied her legs together with the rope. Then he tied her hands, so tight she cried out. The rope dug into her skin and burned when she tried to move. It was useless to struggle. He had her where he wanted her.

Then, he pulled a roll of tape from the pocket of his baggy pants and tore off a long piece. When he moved toward Gloria with it, she recoiled away reflexively. He lunged, smoothing the tape over her mouth.

All the while, he hardly looked at her. While he worked the rope, he looked down, or off to the side. The mumbling grew louder. Now she could make out some of the words. He kept muttering about how he'd make someone pay. They would be sorry. He'd show them. Gloria couldn't imagine what any of it had to do with her. All she knew was that she felt more terror than she ever had in her life.

She took deep breaths through her nose, but they did no good to calm her. Nothing seemed to slow the rapid pounding of her heart. Sunlight filtered through the broken roof of the barn, lighting her captor's hair until it burned gold. Yet it cast his face in shadow, making him look even more menacing as he paced to and fro before her.

Tears streamed down her face, which she wished would stop since she was getting stuffed up and couldn't breathe through her mouth. Calm down. Calm down. It was useless. There was no calming down, not even the threat of suffocating was enough to settle her.

He had to be insane. He paced and paced, mumbling louder, punching his fist into his other palm. Gloria shivered at the thought of that fist making contact with her. She whimpered again without intending to.

"Are you ever going to shut up? Stop crying!" The sound of his voice made her jump. He was so, so angry. There was rage in his voice. He's insane, she thought. She was more sure than ever that this was the man who killed her family. He seemed to have it in him, the rage and instability. But why?

"Do you know who I am?" He laughed a little, almost hysterically, when he asked. He must have known the answer. How could she know who he was?

She took as deep a breath as she could and shook her head.

"That doesn't surprise me." He snorted, shaking his head. Then he turned away for a moment, running his hands through his blonde hair almost frantically. He was sweating, flushed, the shirt sticking to his sweat-stained skin.

He turned back. "Why would anybody tell you? I've been the dirty little secret for so long. My entire life." He walked to her, his footsteps ominous. She braced herself.

"Don't I look like him? The hair, especially. I always thought the hair was a giveaway. That specific color blonde." Gloria recoiled at his nearness. What could he be talking about? Who was "him"?

"Or maybe the nose. We have the same nose. Or, had. I still have it. I imagine his is gone now." Gloria stared at her captor with wide eyes, the meaning behind his words still veiled. He truly was insane, rambling on about things that made no sense.

"Have you figured it out yet? Come on. You're supposed to be such a smart girl. That cop thought so. Or maybe not. Maybe it wasn't his smarts you were after. Englischers and Amish have been known to get together, you know. It happens. I should know, shouldn't I?" He snorted.

Then he stood up straight, sneering down at her.

"I'm your cousin."

Gloria's eyes went wide. She couldn't speak, of course, but even if she could there would have been a loss for words. Her cousin? How could there be a cousin she'd never heard of? She searched her memory for the story of a family member who'd left the order and came up blank. Then again, would her family have told her even if there was such a person? It had become clear that they didn't wish to reveal much to her.

"Don't bother trying to figure it out," he said, smirking. "I'm the dirty little secret, remember? Nobody knew about me. Well…one person did, actually."

Gloria stopped focusing on his shocking announcement and took another good look at him. This time, she studied him, all panic pushed aside. Could it be?

The more she looked, the clearer it became. He was a little heavier, for sure, and his face had more softness to it. The jaw wasn't as sharp, the chin not as square. But the nose was the same. And the hair. And the shape of the eyes, if not the color. The curve of the mouth.

She was looking at a younger version of her Uncle Isaac.

It was breathtaking, the realization, and she gasped sharply once the pieces fell into place. The way he'd called Susan "sister". The way Isaac had shut down any possibility of threat from the young man. He'd wanted them to forget all about it. Gloria finally understood why, and the understanding was enough to turn her stomach.

"You're getting it now, huh? Maybe you really are smart. My name is Andrew King. Nice to meet you." He laughed, the hysterical note still present in his voice. He began to pace in front of her, frantic energy pouring from him.

"I didn't understand, at first," he muttered. "Why was the man with the beard and the hat always visiting? He would come around once a week. My mother used to make up excuses about him. He was selling something, or fixing something, or helping her with something else. And he was handy around the house, too, which helped. Once, he even fixed my rocking horse." He laughed bitterly. "He might have made it, for all I know."

Andrew shook his head. "It's no way for a kid to grow up. Single mother, no other kids in the house, nothing ever mentioned about a father. When I asked why I didn't have a dad like the other kids, mom would never tell me. She never had anything to say. Not even a made-up story. She just told me I didn't have a father, that he was far away now. Nothing else. Nothing about the person he was before he went away, or that he loved me and wished he could be with me. All the fairytale stuff kids need to hear, you know? She could have at least tried to give that to me."

So much anger. He had such a deep, violent anger which Gloria couldn't begin to fathom. Another thing she couldn't fathom was growing up without a father. What must it have been like? Not that his absent father gave Andrew the right to do what he was doing, but it had probably contributed to his instability.

"The other kids would make fun of me all the time. I didn't have a dad, my mom was always working. I might as well have lived alone. I was so alone. Even when Mom was home, she was sleeping between shifts at her jobs. I raised myself for the most part. Do you know how that feels?" He turned to glare at her. She was too afraid of him to make a move in any direction. He sneered again. "Of course, you don't. Your life has been perfect, just like his life was. Faith and family and community. Happy. Safe. Loved. It must be nice. I wouldn't know."

He pummeled the palm of his hand again, his agitation increasing. Gloria's eyes swept left and right, searching for a weapon to use if the moment came. How would she use it, though? Her ankles were bound so tight; she would only be able to hop. Her feet were going slightly numb, too, so there was no telling whether she would be able to get anywhere even if she did hop. And her hands were also numb, the rope tight enough to cut off circulation. She moved her wrists all she should, wincing from the rough rope burn but desperately trying to keep blood flowing.

"When I got older, I started paying attention. I noticed the way they spoke to each other, Mom and the stranger-who-wasn't-a-stranger. I still saw him every week, but he was a mystery. I always liked mysteries. I would hang around where they couldn't see me and listen in. They didn't talk like strangers. They talked like they knew each other very, very well. Better than they should have, you know? Sometimes they talked about me. He would ask questions about how I was doing in school and whether I was healthy and happy. Mom always lied and told him I was happy. Then again, how would she know? I never told her I wasn't."

He let out something between a roar and a cry of pain. "I hated it. I hated the way she'd get so excited when he was about to come over. She'd clean up the house and put on a nice dress, and she'd sit there with him like there was nothing wrong. It felt like she waited all week for him. Once he was gone, she'd get sad again. But she would never tell me why."

"One day, I'd had enough. I couldn't take it any more, you know? The way they acted like I was a kid. I think I was sixteen by then —maybe I was still a kid, mostly, but I knew enough about the world. And I asked them while they sat together who he was to me. I asked if he was my father. I saw enough of a resemblance between us by then. Especially the hair. Mom is a redhead. I wondered sometimes where my blonde hair came from, and once, when he took of his hat, I saw his hair was the same color."

"They looked at each other. Neither of them knew what to say.

What was there to say, I guess? They couldn't lie. I knew enough to know he was something. Know what I mean? He wasn't just a random stranger. He had a connection to me."

"So, finally, he told me the truth. He was my father."

Andrew stopped pacing, frozen stiff, like he'd just heard the news for the first time. "I didn't know what to think. My father? This man? I thought my father was far away. I used to make up all kinds of stories about the person he was. You know?" He looked at Gloria. "No, you probably don't know. I used to dream that he was a spy, working for the government. Or in the military. Or on a secret mission as a scientist, studying ancient tribes to unlock the keys to life." He chuckled. "I watched a lot of movies."

"And there he was," Andrew continued. "This plain, Amish man. Who didn't know who the Amish were? And he was my father. It was unreal. I asked a million questions—of course, hardly any of them got answered. One did, though. I asked him if he had another family. He said yes."

He laughed, a sharp, barking laugh that sent chills down Gloria's spine. "He said yes. He had a family of his own. A wife. A daughter. Two sons. My brothers and sister."

Gloria's heart clenched at the memory of her cousins. So this was why they died.

"I wanted to meet them, of course. I was dying to. I finally understood why it always felt like there was a missing piece of me. I never felt whole inside. I know it sounds stupid, and maybe I'm kidding myself into thinking it, but I don't think I am. I knew there was more of me out there, more people like me. People who would accept me and understand me. They wouldn't tell me I was being too much, like mom did. They wouldn't look at me funny, the way my teachers did. And they would be my friends. I would finally have friends. I was never good at keeping them. But siblings would have to stick around, because we'd be related. They wouldn't have a choice but to be my friend."

"I used to think about them all the time. Once my father told me they existed. What were they like? Their lives had to be so different, you know? I had movies and TV and games and stuff. What did they have? I did all the research I could on the Amish, the way they lived and dressed and spoke. I saved up my allowance and bought a set of plain clothes—the dark pants, the plain shirt, suspenders. A hat. The next time my father came around, I put them on to show him. I could be just like him. I wanted him to see how I could be like him, how I could fit into that world."

Andrew shook his head. "You know what he said? He said it could never be. It would never be. I didn't understand what it meant to be Amish. Then he said a bunch of other words. I had to understand, he told me."

Those dark, angry eyes found Gloria again, and the depth of rage in them was almost too much for her to bear. Her heart took off at a gallop.

"You know what I heard, though? Behind his words? That I was good enough for him. For you people. He was ashamed of me. That's why nobody could know about me. He had to keep me hidden away, like I was something dirty. Meanwhile, he could live his life like nothing happened. Is that fair? That people loved him and trusted him, when he had a family on the side?"

Gloria didn't know what to think. It still seemed so unreal, the idea of Uncle Isaac carrying on with a woman. An Englischer, at that. It was the sort of thing that only happened in that outside world, or so she'd believed. All those years of keeping a second family secret. What must it have done to him? It couldn't have been easy, the guilt and shame he must have felt. It wasn't totally unfounded. He'd sinned, for sure.

And his family paid for it.

"I hated him from that moment on. I made it a point to not be around when he came around. I didn't want to see him. He didn't get to show up once a week and expect me to be happy to see him. He was a liar, and he left us. He didn't even give Mom money to take care of me—if he did, it wasn't much. But then I guess you people don't make all that much money. What do I know? All I know is, we suffered for what he did. And the hatred grew inside me, you know?"

"I couldn't stop thinking about my brothers and sister, though. I made up names for them, I gave them personalities. I even made up stories in my head about things we did together when we were little. Fights we had and good times, too. It was so much nicer to think about that than to face my life. That second life was much better. I would look for any excuse to go back to it. Sometimes I would stay in bed for days, pretending I was there with my siblings instead of in my actual life. Mom got so worried about me. I couldn't tell the doctors the truth about what I was doing. They would think I was crazy."

And they'd be right, Gloria thought. She didn't know if the insanity started because he obsessed over his other family, or if it was present before that. He'd mentioned being "too much", not having any friends. Maybe he was always slightly off, and this pushed him over the edge.

"I started following Susan. First, I had to find out where the family lived. I trailed after my father one day when he left my house, riding my bike. It's not hard to keep up with a buggy. I saw him stop off at an Amish store. I watched through the window. Everybody liked him. They all said hello and asked how he was doing. They asked about his family. I could tell they respected him. Oh, you have no idea how badly I wanted to run in there and tell them all the truth. He wasn't the good man they thought he was. He was a hypocrite, posing as a faithful, pious person. He'd had an affair with my mother. I wondered what they would think about that."

"But I didn't. I don't know why. Maybe it was because I didn't want my brothers and sister to go through the stuff I went through. It would be hardest on them. So I stayed quiet and followed him home."

"I followed him everywhere after that. I learned the names of my siblings. Susan was so pretty, wasn't she? She laughed all the time."

Gloria's heart sank. How long had he been watching? Longer than she'd known. He'd only made himself visible in the last few years, but this seemed to reach back further than that.

"Then, I started following her to the farmer's market. I don't know why she interested me the most. Maybe because we were around the same age—the boys were so much younger. That was a little disappointing. I had hoped they were closer to me, so we might have been better friends."

You would never have been friends, Gloria thought with real bitterness. They would have seen through you.

"Do you remember the first time we saw each other there? You and me, cousin? I do. And I was so happy to find out that I had cousins, too. You have a big family, don't you? So many more people to know and be close with. It was too good to be true. I was so happy to know that you were out there, that there was more of my family in the world. I wanted to know you better, too, but it wasn't as easy. Your house wasn't as close to the main road as my father's house, and you had a big dog that might have seen me. Do you still have that dog?"

Gloria nodded. His mind was gone. He was going all over the place. Asking about her dog, as though they knew each other. How shocking, knowing that he'd followed her and knew so much about her life. She should have told her Daed about him, instead of leaving it to Uncle Isaac. But he had always been so wise, she'd looked up to him so much. If she had only second-guessed him, just once, tragedy might have been avoided.

"I only wanted to talk to her. I only wanted to tell her she was my sister, and I loved her. Because I did! I did love her. I loved my entire family. I couldn't stand on the outside anymore. You can't stand on the outside when you love people as long as I loved them. I didn't love my father—any hope of that died when he rejected me, told me I wasn't good enough to be like him. I didn't understand his faith. I forgot about him after that. He would never love me. But the rest? I wanted to be closer to them for real. I wanted my second life to be my first life. I only wanted to talk."

Andrew's face twisted into a snarl. "But no. She wouldn't. She was still too good for me. She ran away, with you. And I knew, then. I knew I would have to end it. I didn't love her anymore. I hated her, too. I would make her pay. They would all pay."

Gloria let out a heartbroken whimper. It was all too tragic. This sick, twisted person and his obsession. He could have been stopped, if only somebody had known enough to stop him. Her aunt and cousins had died for no reason. So had her uncle, but it was difficult to be as forgiving as she knew she should. His actions had Gotten his family killed. They were innocent.

"I remember the night I did it," Andrew said, oblivious to the pain he was causing his cousin. Or maybe he knew, and just didn't care. Maybe he took pleasure in telling every detail, knowing it was like a knife in his cousin's heart. "I poured gasoline all around the place and struck a match. It was that easy. The house went up like a pile of dry kindling—it was all wood, but you know that, of course. Everybody was asleep. It took no time before the place was engulfed. I stood back and watched, from the fields. Pretty soon everybody came running from the farms all around, and I sneaked away before they could find me. The whole thing took maybe five minutes from beginning to end."

To hear him talk about it so coolly, callously, sent pain through Gloria's body. She felt herself collapsing a little under the weight of his words. The images they called to mind. That house, the one she had nearly grown up in, going up so quickly. Taking the lives of the people she held dear. It took almost no time. The only comfort was knowing they couldn't have suffered long. Tears ran down her face again.

She was surprised to see tears rolling down Andrew's cheeks, too. "It didn't have to be that way! If he had only loved me instead of hiding me away like I was trash he was ashamed of! He could have been good to me. He could have. But no. he was too full of himself and his own goodness! He loved his other family so much more! They were worth it to him. I wasn't. My mom wasn't. He would never love us the way a father is supposed to love his family! I'm glad he's dead," he spat. "I'm glad. He deserves it for what he did to us. And for the lies he told his wife and my cousins, and the whole community who thought he was so great. He burned, the way he should have burned for his sins."

Gloria continued to cry, feeling like her heart was being ripped from her chest. It was too much, all of it. And to hear Andrew tell it with such desperation and hatred made the whole thing even worse.

The worst was yet to come, though. Andrew stood in front of Gloria, tilting his head to the side. She shrank beneath his gaze.

"I'm sorry to have to do this to you." With that, he reached into the waistband of his pants and pulled out a gun. Gloria shrieked behind the tape, the sound muffled. She wriggled in her bonds, but it was no use. There was no getting away from a gun.

"I don't want to have to hurt you," he said, more tears rolling down his cheeks. "But you shouldn't have Gotten together with that detective. Who knows what will happen now? All I know is, I can't let you talk to him again. It's too risky. Why couldn't you mind your own business? None of this would have happened. You'd be home right now, with your family. Now I have to kill you. I'm really sorry, Gloria."

This was it. This was how she was going to die. Her entire short life had led up to this moment. She squeezed her eyes shut, praying that death would come quickly and painlessly, and that Gott would take her into His kingdom. The faces of her family floated through her consciousness, and she wished she might have had time to say goodbye. The last thing she told them was a lie. Would she be punished for that after death came? Why had she lied?

Mamm won't be able to take it, she thought. It will be too much for her to bear. Her heart broke, imagining the fresh pain that would sweep over her already grieving family.

This is how I'm going to die. This is how I'm going to die. Oh, please, let it be a dream. But it was no dream.

"I'm sorry, Gloria," he said again. "Say hello to my brothers and sister for me."

She squeezed her eyes more tightly shut, waiting for the sound of the shot and the feeling of hot lead tearing through her body.

A loud crashing sound. Not the sound of a shot. A crashing sound.

Gloria dared to open her eyes. Sunlight streamed into the barn. The door had been broken open, and a half-dozen men came streaming into the barn. They screamed, their voices fighting one another to be heard. They commanded Andrew to drop his weapon, to put his hands up. It was almost scarier than Andrew's tirade, until Gloria finally registered understanding that the men were there to save her. They were policemen.

Paul! He came rushing into the barn behind his men and went straight to her. "I'm sorry it took so long," he said, working at the rope which bound her hands and feet. "It's a miracle we found this place."

Gloria cried too hard to understand much of what Paul was saying. It was enough to see him kneeling before her. He had come for her. He saved her. She was on the verge of drawing her last breath when he saved her.

He did his best to pull the tape from her mouth gently, but it still pulled and hurt. She didn't care. Her heart was too full of relief to feel much pain.

"How did you know?" she asked, breathless, shaking with sobs.

"Come on. Let's get out of here, first. I'm taking you to the police station to make a statement, and then I'll take you home."

"My parents!"

"They know." He placed a hand over hers, and she didn't think to withdraw it. "I sent one of my men to the house. They might already be at the station by the time we get there."

Her parents at a police station. It seemed too strange to be believed. She allowed Paul to help her out of the barn, her feet and legs still shaky and a little numb from being tied for so long. He helped her into his car and they sped off toward the station.

"How did you know?" she asked again, taking deep breaths of fresh air. She would never take life for granted again. It was like she'd been given a second chance.

"It was the 'sister' thing. It got me thinking. I couldn't stop thinking all last night, so I did some research into your uncle. As it turns out, the house Andrew and his mother lived in was purchased by Isaac King not long before Andrew's birth. It didn't take much to put two and two together."

"How did you find me at the barn?"

"Several witnesses saw him drive away with you. We got a few phone calls. One of them even gave us the license plate of the car. We had cars patrolling the entire area, looking for you or at least the car. One of them spotted it at the barn."

It was sheer luck, then. That was what had saved her. No—it was Gott. Only Gott could have put things in motion that way. The witnesses who took the time to call, the officers who took the time to look for her so thoroughly.

And Paul, who figured out that Andrew was her cousin.

She noticed the way his hands shook slightly as they gripped the wheel of the car. "Are you all right?" she asked.

He glanced at her and laughed in surprise. "Leave it to you to ask me if I'm doing all right, when you're the one who was almost killed. Yes. I'm fine. Just very, very relieved."

"So am I," she answered. Words couldn't possibly convey how relieved she felt, and how deeply grateful she was to Gott for bringing her to safety.

She looked out the window at what would have been an ordinary day. A beautiful one by any standards, but even more beautiful in Gloria's eyes. She would never take an ordinary Fall day for granted again.

It was an ordinary Fall day. The sky was a brilliant blue, the sort of blue that only appears on crisp October days. The leaves were changing, studding the landscape with deep gold's and rich reds. It was enough to take a person's breath away, and Gloria stood in awe of the day's beauty before stepping off her front porch and walking to the main road.

The little chill in the air was a delight, and it promised an even chillier evening. She loved nothing more than sitting with the family around the hearth. Mamm would work on stitching, Daed would smoke his pipe and read the Bible. The rest would busy themselves in other ways. Gloria would invariably work on a new quilt, the fabric spread out over the kitchen table. Her needle would fly in the light of the oil lamp, and she would laugh and joke with her brothers and sisters as she worked. It was something she looked forward to, even as she delighted in the day's majesty.

She made her walk to town, as she had so many times before. The rest of the world spun on as it always did. Tourists went to and fro, speeding by in their cars. Music blared out the open windows. A few of them even stared at her. She was getting better accustomed to their stares and no longer held it against them. They couldn't help themselves. Just another way she had found a new depth of maturity in the face of adversity. Another one of Gott's hidden blessings.

It was a normal day for the tourists, as it was for the occasional Amish man or woman she bid good day to as she walked to the souvenir shop. In many ways it was a normal day for her, too. She'd woken up before dawn as always. She'd done her chores— making beds, washing dishes, sweeping floors, hanging clothes to dry. She'd eaten breakfast around the table with her family, as she had so many times before. It was a day like any other.

Only it wasn't. It had been exactly one year since Andrew King abducted her. The memory of that day seemed to hang above her like a grim reminder of how very different things might have turned out. If the police had been just a half-minute later in breaking open the door, Gloria wouldn't be enjoying a walk on a beautiful day. It seemed impossible, the way life could hinge on the briefest moments.

The few days leading up to the anniversary were solemn ones. Mamm had been a little sad, a little teary-eyed. There was no escaping the pain, though it had greatly diminished over a year's time. The shock and horror had softened. Now, it was only a matter of missing loved ones. It was one thing that they were gone, but another that they had died so needlessly. It was one of Gott's great mysteries, for sure. The way such good people could be taken down by such evil.

Was Andrew evil? Gloria had asked herself the question many times, and she had talked about it with Paul during his many visits to check on her. He'd wanted to be sure she recovered fully from the experience. Together they had worked out her feelings toward her cousin.

He wasn't evil, she decided. He'd done an evil deed, but that didn't make him evil. He was very sick, very twisted. His mother had been devastated when she learned of his crimes, and admitted to police that her son had been troubled for many years. It was clear to Gloria from the way he described his life. He was already sick, and his obsession with his father and siblings had escalated that illness until he exploded in an act of evil.

Now he was in prison, and would be for a long time. Gloria prayed for him every day, that he would be able to get well while he was there. Paul had assured her that her cousin would receive the help he needed from doctors at the prison. By the time he was released, he might be able to try for a normal life. If it was Gott's will, it would be so.

Another thing she and Paul discussed often was Isaac's double life. It had come as a great shock to the community when the truth of his secret was revealed. Literally no one had any idea of it. He'd been very careful to keep the two sides of his life separate. Only the deed to the little house in which Andrew grew up revealed the truth.

She stepped into the souvenir shop and said hello to the owners. They discussed an order for new quilts, which Gloria assured them they would get before the holiday rush started. She had so many things which kept her life full and busy, and she thanked Gott every day for each of them.

A stop at the farmer's market nearly brought tears to her eyes. She saw the stand at which she and Susan used to sell produce to customers. Now, her sisters took care of the booth. She said hello to them and passed some time chatting, running her hands over the wood of the booth where she and Susan had passed so many happy hours together, giggling over secrets and teasing each other. There was a hole in her heart now, one which would never completely be filled. It was more manageable all the time, though. That was the beauty of faith. It helped those who had it get through even the darkest of times.

After saying goodbye to her sisters, Gloria had one more stop to make. She hurried across the street to the coffee shop, hoping she wasn't too late.

If she was, he didn't seem to care. His warm smile light up the room when she appeared.

"Sorry," she said, taking a seat at their usual table. "A bigger-than-usual order for quilts."

"Does this mean I won't be seeing as much of you while you work?" Paul asked, grinning. She shook her head in mock disappointment.

"You know how important my work is. I wouldn't tell you to take time away from yours."

"True. I guess I have to give you the same consideration." He was only teasing, of course, and Gloria giggled.

"I ordered for you," he said. "Your usual."

"One day I want to be really different and try one of the fancy drinks," she said, sipping her iced coffee.

"You're not missing much." His drink was plain, like hers. A lot had changed in only a year.

"How has your day been?" she asked.

"The usual. I'm worried about the chickens. They're not growing as they should."

"Did you try the special feed Mr. Stoltzfus gave you?"

"Yes," he said. "I'll give it a few more days before I decide the old man is a little too confident in his feed." He grinned, taking her hand from across the table. "It's coming back to me, slowly but surely."

"You'll get there," Gloria assured him. "It's like riding a bike, I guess. You have knowledge of the land, and how things grow and work together. That's a good start. The rest will come back."

"You're right. You're always right." His smile flashed at her above his beard. He was just as handsome to her as he was when they first met, back when he lived among the Englischers. Over the year between their first meeting and their morning at the coffee shop, much had changed.

Sometimes Gloria wondered whether Paul would come to regret returning to his Amish roots. Life seemed so much easier for the Englischers. They didn't have the challenges of simple life. At first, when he declared his intention to return to the faith, she'd been skeptical of his intentions.

He'd proven himself over time, however, to the point where even the bishop was convinced that Paul meant every word of his heartfelt plea to be baptized into the faith. Since then, every day was better than the one before. Gloria could feel free to fall in love with Paul. And she did, head over heels.

They left the shop together, arm-in-arm. It was still such a thrill to be with him. He was a man of honor and nobility, and he worked tirelessly to make his farm a success. It was sort of an understanding between them that once the farm was running smoothly the two of the would be married. With that in mind, Gloria was never too busy to give advice or help him with anything he needed. Her Daed helped, too, often visiting with his sons to lend a hand. Everyone worked together to ensure Paul and Gloria's happiness.

There was no way to live a life of such joy outside the faith. Gloria was sure of this. Nowhere else could a family be so close. Nowhere else did neighbors help one another as though they were family. They all depended on one another, and they worked together for something greater than themselves. And all of it was for the glory of Gott, and all according to His will.

"May I drive you home?" Paul asked, gesturing toward his buggy. Gloria smiled up into the face of the man she loved and nodded, thanking Gott for His many blessings.

I would like to thank you for taking the time to read my book. I really hope that you enjoyed it as much as I enjoyed writing it.

I have been writing Amish books for Amazon for almost two years now, almost exclusively on Kindle. However, due to growing demand I managed to get the majority of my titles available in paperback versions. There is a list of all of my kindle books below, bit by bit they are ALL going to be released in paperback so please keep checking them.

If you feel able I would love for you to give the book a short review on Amazon.

If you want to keep up to date with all of my latest releases then please like my Facebook Page, simply search for Hannah Schrock author.

Many thanks once again, all my love.

Hannah.

LATEST BOOKS

DON'T MISS HANNAH'S BRAND NEW *MAMMOTH AMISH MEGA BOOK* - 20 Stories in one box set.

[Mammoth Amish Romance Mega Book 20 books in one set](#)

Outstanding value for 20 books

OTHER BOX SETS

[Amish Romance Mega book](#) **(contains many of Hannah's older titles)**

[Amish Love and Romance Collection](#)

MOST RECENT SINGLE TITLES

The Orphan's Amish Teacher

The Mysterious Amish Suicide

The Pregnant Amish Quilt Maker

The Amish Caregiver

The Amish Detective: The King Family Arsonist

The Amish Gift

Becoming Amish

The Amish Foundling Girl

The Heartbroken Amish Girl

The Missing Amish Girl

Amish Joy

The Amish Detective

Amish Double

The Burnt Amish Girl

AMISH ROMANCE SERIES

AMISH HEARTACHE

AMISH REFLECTIONS: AMISH ANTHOLOGY COLLECTION

MORE AMISH REFLECTIONS : ANOTHER AMISH ANTHOLOGY COLLECTION

THE AMISH WIDOW AND THE PREACHER'S SON

AN AMISH CHRISTMAS WITH THE BONTRAGER SISTERS

A BIG BEAUTIFUL AMISH COURTSHIP

AMISH YOUNG SPRING LOVE BOX SET

AMISH PARABLES SERIES BOX SET

AMISH HEART SHORT STORY COLLECTION

AMISH HOLDUP

AN AMISH TRILOGY BOX SET

AMISH ANGUISH

SHORT AMISH ROMANCE STORIES

AMISH BONTRAGER SISTERS 2 - THE COMPLETE SECOND SEASON

AMISH BONTRAGER SISTERS - THE COMPLETE FIRST SEASON

THE AMISH BROTHER'S BATTLE

AMISH OUTSIDER

AMISH FORGIVENESS AND FRIENDSHIP

THE AMISH OUTSIDER'S LIE

AMISH VANITY

AMISH NORTH

AMISH YOUNG SPRING LOVE SHORT STORIES SERIES

[THE AMISH BISHOP'S DAUGHTER](#)

[AN AMISH ARRANGEMENT](#)

[AMISH REJECTION](#)

[AMISH BETRAYAL](#)

THE AMISH BONTRAGER SISTERS SHORT STORIES SERIES

[AMISH RETURN](#)

[AMISH BONTRAGER SISTERS COMPLETE COLLECTION](#)

[AMISH APOLOGY](#)

[AMISH UNITY](#)

[AMISH DOUBT](#)

AMISH FAMILY

THE ENGLISCHER'S GIFT

AMISH SECRET

AMISH PAIN

THE AMISH PARABLES SERIES

THE AMISH BUILDER

THE AMISH PRODIGAL SON

AMISH PERSISTENCE

THE AMISH GOOD SAMARITAN

Also Out Now:

The Amish Gift

Rebecca Beiler has always longed and prayed for motherhood but fate decides something else for her as she suffers her second miscarriage. Torn and heartbroken, Rebecca finds herself questioning her faith and has trouble coping with the loss until one day she finds a remarkable gift - a newborn baby.

Restoring their faith in Gott, Rebecca and her husband James believe this child is a gift from Gott. After a fruitless search for the child's parents, they take her as their own and name her Eve. But will Gott let them keep this miracle baby? What will be the fate of young Eve? Will her real mother return to claim her back? Can Rebecca and James ever have the happy family they so deeply deserve and long for?

A charming, clean and wholesome new Amish romance story from Hannah Schrock, full of joy and heartache, but does it have a happy ending?

Here is a Taster:

Rebecca drummed her fingers against the cold of the window sill - her brilliant emerald eyes now vacant with the possibility of could-be but never was. A small hastened breath escaped her lips in the form of a sigh and her vacant stare kept cutting across the image before her but she did not see anything – all else was irrelevant except the gut wrenching twisting of the knife in the bottom of her grief.

They say each person deals with grief in their own way and Rebecca knew the stages all too well. It starts off with a sense of denial that stems from the very core of your mind and stretches out all the way to the ends of your fingertips – it's a state of stupefaction where you know the event around you is happening but it just fails to register insides the confines of your brain. Denial.

But the ignorant bliss of denial is not long lived – like everything, it passes. And with it comes a surge of all the sensations you had been avoiding – the flood after the bursting of the dam. It's all consuming and you cannot escape the anger it dissipates in its wake.

You ask why when you find yourself kneeled to prayer in the middle of the night and you are questioning Gott and you're sobbing. The first time it happened - Rebecca remembers all too well still. Her husband James had been there and he had comforted her when she felt like the darkness of the night had been far too much to cope, he held her hand and told her it is only what Gott wanted.

Rebecca believed him and then slowly, the depression started to alleviate – the Lord answered her pleas and took away her pain. It started to become easier to breathe – it took months and too many tears to count but He answered and acceptance swept over Rebecca.

That was the first time it happened.

Another sigh and more rhythmic drumming of the fingers – a tactic to divert the mind away from what it pressed on it the most, the urge not to peel away the top layer of skin after a fresh wound – you know it would only hurt more but the temptation is too strong to resist.

Rebecca Beiler found herself blinking back the tears as the events of last night came flooding back to her – the proverbial skin of the wound being peeled.

It had been a bright day and Rebecca and James Beiler could not have even imagined the gale of the tragedy that was about to hit them. Truth was, the atmosphere was happy and gay as the Beiler couple expected the birth of their boppli. It was an exciting moment in their life and Rebecca had daydreamed of giving birth to her own so to finally complete their familye – a vision engraved in her brain for two years ever since they had gotten married.

The first time – though – it did not turn out so well. Rebecca had suffered a miscarriage early into her first pregnancy and the loss had left her devastated but slowly, she recovered. This time, though, she was certain that this pregnancy would not share the same fate as her last. For one thing, she was far ahead in her pregnancy than she had been before. This time, she knew Gott had listened to her pleas for a familye and He would not disappoint her.

And so when it happened, it was all the more heartbreaking.

James and Rebecca had been sitting in recluse after carrying out their activities for the day – they felt exhausted and were simply spending some quality time with the other for relaxation. That is when it happened.

Rebecca felt a sharp pain in her belly all of a sudden – the kind of pain that brings you down to your knees to grovel, her hand flying down to her plump belly and her eyes shutting in immense agony, screams escaping her mouth. James was by her side in an instant – holding back her hair, comforting her but the pain did not stop – it refused to cease and her screams only grew louder as she writhed on the room floor.

Next thing she knew; she was being transported to Englischer hospital. A flurry of rushed physicians and panic spreading the room; Rebecca thought she was going into early labor but should she be so lucky. Through bated breaths and the sheer will to stay conscious, she saw what had conspired. The blood – the blood was everywhere. The pain was unrelenting and Rebecca knew far too well what it all meant.

"I am sorry, you have lost the baby," the Englischer doctor told her a few hours later and Rebecca felt as though she had been struck hard by a thousand lightning bolts all at once.

Of course, James was by her side – holding her hand and comforting her, whispering comforting verses from the Book to her. But there was no escaping the dread of the hollow the unborn boppli had left behind in its wake – she never even got to hear its sweet laughter or even have it grab her hand with its tiny fingers.

She thought she has endured the most difficult time of her life when the first miscarriage happened but evidently, the second one proved that the first was just a trail run – incomparable compared to the real deal, for this time was far more intense than she could ever imagine even bearing. Yet here she was in the midst of it all.

That night, there had been incontrollable sobbing and insomnia as the reality set in – Rebecca had just lost her another shot at the perfect family she had dreamt of having for the past three years.

Two days later the doctors deemed her healthy enough to be discharged and her and James returned to their haus. The health they had prescribed her to have was perhaps only physical as she still felt as wretched and horrible as day one – the heartbreak was real and it was unimaginable.

Forward to now, as Rebecca still stands in front of the same window sill, her mind having recounted the events. Looking up to the sky outside, she wondered how high she would have to mount herself to be able to see Gott – surely, He lived up in the great big sky. The thoughts coming to Rebecca were automatic and thus out of her control – which is what she tried to tell herself before she quickly dismissed them.

But as more and more time kept passing, she realized just like there was no escaping the pain, there was also no escaping the intrusive thoughts that refused to leave her lonesome.

Twenty-five-year-old Rebecca Beiler was of course quite a sturdy believer of Gott – she thought obstacles only came to the special ones and only served to strengthen her belief in Gott – or at least that was what she had been taught for all her life in the early preaching's of her Mamm and Daed.

Now however, for the first time in her life, she felt her faith being shaken.

Prostrating before the invisible Gott she so adamantly believed in all her life, she raised her hands once more time and nothing but a broken sob escaped her lips. She could not even bring herself to formulate words out but they stung like a broken glass deep in her heart.

Hearing her sobs grow louder, James suddenly rushed to her side from the other room.

"Rebecca!" he called out to her, kneeling down besides her at once, "are you alright?" If James had proved to be anything throughout this entire episode and the one before it, it was that he was indeed a very devoted husband who did not ever want to see his fraa upset with anything. It literally brought him pain to see his fraa in such a condition..

At once, Rebecca lazily wiped away some of the stray tears and then nodded. "Jah," she said quietly, "I am gut." However, the vacant hollowness of her eyes gave away that she was indeed anything but.

"I am worried for you," James said, his tone soft as he examined the moisture laden face of his fraa, "Please, I know it has been hard but we must learn to move on, as a familye."

His words were meant to be comforting but at the current moment, they proved to be anything but as a fresh batch of salty tears came cascading down her cheeks as soon he uttered that last word.

"Familye?" she repeated through the tears, "Ach, I am not worthy to be considered to be part of one. I keep failing and failing – Gott keeps taking away what is rightfully mine."

Even James was surprised to hear such a bold accusation from Rebecca who was usually so pious and steadfast. Still, he understood it was only her grief talking and instead put a helping arm behind her back for support.

"Gott works in mysterious ways, Rebecca," he said to her softly, "He must have a plan for us," he reassured.

But the grief of losing her boppli had left such a massive hole in its wake that the seed of doubt had been planted before there could even be any resistance. For the first time in her life, she was questioning Gott's plans for her and His intentions.

"What plans?" she called out in agony, "Why me? I did not deserve this – I am a pious woman of good. So why did He do this to me? Ach, why does He keep doing this to me? The first time it happened, I thought I would die of the pain. But I lived on – because I thought He would never be too cruel and His test would end. But what now? Why did I have to endure it again?" she ranted, tears now flowing freely down her sides.

But before James could even formulate a reply, Rebecca was at it again, "I do not see why I have to endure this. Does He not know just badly I want a familye for us? How badly I wanted to be a mamm. The doctor said it would have been a dochder – now I will dream of her every night and she will live on in my memory forever," the words were flowing freely out of Rebecca's mouth now and she was surprised at her own ability to utter them but still, that did not make it stop.

"I have asked Him for a familye – relentlessly each time I sit down to pray. Why does He not listen?" a broken sob encapsulated the end of the sentence.

James was patient, "Stop now, you are not talking sense," he said but made it a point not to sound harsh in his assessment, " Gott knows what we do not. Take comfort in His wisdom," he said, wrapping both his arms around her tightly to pull her into a hug. She let herself be comforted and then she sobbed and sobbed and sobbed.

--

The next few days were a haze and a blur as Rebecca continued on with the normalcy of daily life, now having been completely healed from the wounds of the miscarriage. However, the heart still ached and it resulted into an odd concoction of her being alive but doing it in such a state of numbness that it would almost be fair to call her absent. She had been lulled into a form of conscious comatose and finally, James decided he had seen enough suffering and decided to confront her one afternoon.

"Rebecca," he called out from the door as he caught his fraa in another one of her episodes where she just dropped every other task and stared vacantly to what was ahead of her for hours.

"Rebecca!" the second time he called out was louder and it seemed to do the job as she snapped out of her midday daze.

"Ach!" she said as her mind got transported back to the present, "my apologies, I must have just- well,' she found herself tongue-tied and instead looked up to her husband, hoping that her eyes could convey what her words could not.

Of course, he understood her better than anybody else and did not need any verbal communication to confirm his doubts about the reason behind his fraa's current state of bereavement.

"I am so worried for you," he said to her and you could hear the concern laced in his tone, "this is nee gut – you have become a shell of the woman you were before and I am worried sick at the prospect of you growing worse. Please – communicate with me."

They say at the lowest point, when all bets are off and negotiations have suspended, a man is beaten down to begging. And that was exactly what James was doing as he grabbed her hands and forced her to look at him with her vacant green eyes.

"Please," he beseeched once again.

The woman held his gaze for a few seconds before she broke away and again stared out in front of her. "I am gut. Your concern warms my heart but I do not deserve it," she gulped loudly, "so take solace in the fact that I am okay. Please."

But even to Rebecca, it sounded like she was trying to convince herself more than she could James.

He was shaking his head, "Nee. I will not let you spiral into this state of depression any longer. How come you are like this? The last time –I remember," James stopped to gulp loudly as he recalled the events of her first miscarriage, "the last time – it was easier and you were back to your old self in some days."

A sigh. "This one is different," Harder but she did not let out the last part of that sentence out loud.

"Fine! But I will not stand this any longer! From now on, you must only rest and do nothing else. Suspend all your activities around the house – you are to rest until you are relieved of this massive grief!" James exclaimed.

But instead of his words having been met with relief, Rebecca's eyes widened in horror instead, "Nee. Please. Do not do this – I need the distraction. Doing these chores – the work around the haus – it keeps my brain busy," Rebecca explained, "do not take this away from me or else I will succumb to my own thoughts. Believe me, my mind is not a place I want to be in right now."

James sighed, knowing that she was right. "Have faith in Gott. He will relieve you of this soon."

In spirit of keeping true to the promise Rebecca made her husband, James, of at least trying to snap out of her depression, Rebecca had taken it upon herself to drown herself in work. It seemed that work was the only medicine to her ails of a broken heart – for it provided her with distraction enough to keep her from meditating on the events of her loss.

And so, when she came out to lock the barn one night, she only had work on her mind. Walking over the entrance of it, Rebecca paused for a moment to look around and admire how clear the night sky was today – with the stars all splattered across in and shining in their brilliance.

And that was when she heard a noise.

At first, Rebecca thought it had been a rustle of the wind or perhaps even her own ears playing tricks on her. But when she heard it again, she knew it was none of those things.

The sound was of a soft cooing – whimper almost but not native to any animal she had ever known. In fact, she knew exactly what the sound sounded like but not to get ahead of herself and her possible delusions, she entered the barn to inquire for herself.

It did not take a lot of finding to finally locate the source of the whimpering and the site nearly knocked out the wind out of Rebecca.

Carefully and almost tiptoeing to reach the source, Rebecca loomed closer. The source was a small wicker basket placed on one corner of the barn but what was significant was what was inside the basket.

Wrapped in blankets and bobbing up and down was a boppli and upon seeing it up close finally and having her suspicions confirmed, Rebecca could hardly believe her eyes.

The coos – Rebecca now realized – were actually small whimper of the boppli crying. Panicking at the sight, Rebecca hunched over at once and carefully, almost with trembling arms, picked up the boppli at once.

And there, in her arms, as she slowly rocked it back and forth, Rebecca looked into its for the first time as its crying subsided and realized that it is a girl. And when she looked back at Rebecca, she could hardly do anything else but hug it as tightly to her as she could – her heart swelling up to twice its size.

Standing there, Rebecca realized two things – one: that she had just found an abandoned boppli in her barn and second, she would do whatever she could in her power to keep it safe for as long as she could.

Slowly, shifting the boppli onto the other arm and carefully crunching downwards to pick up the wicker basket, Rebecca began her ascent to back inside the haus.

She did not know what this meant or who the boppli belonged to or why, she of all people had encountered this situation.

But she knew that she had to inform James about the situation this instant.

Looking down at her, Rebecca saw that she had fallen asleep in her arms and the crying had subsided with it. The peaceful sight of slumber nearly made Rebecca's eyes well up with tears.

Indeed, Gott worked in mysterious ways.

--

James heard the thud of the door closing and emerged from the other room to see his fraa but what he saw in her hands was not exactly what he had been expecting. Standing there with his mouth agape from across the room, James stared at his fraa and most importantly, the small bundle of a human she had wrapped up in her arms.

Seeing his obvious shock, Rebecca passed him a look as if to say "this is alright" and walked closer to him.

Still at a loss of words, James stared at her and then back at the boppli – his vision following a sort of a rhythmic oscillation between the two. Finally, he found his voice to speak buried beneath the immense initial shock, "Rebecca, where have you gotten this boppli?" he asked with his eyes widened incredulously.

Rebecca swallowed a lump of saliva she has been harboring in anticipation of her husband's response, "In the barn – she was right there – just left there to fend for herself!" she explained but she could see that the confusion was far from being erased from her husband's face.

"Hey – why are you seeming so worried?" she inquired, her grip on the bundle of blankets tightening as a defense mechanism – the maternal instinct whose use was made obsolete to her a few days ago.

James shook his head wildly, "Forgive me Rebecca but I am more than a little confused at the current state of events – I do not understand – how did you just find a boppli nestled in the middle of our barn?"

The tone that James' voice had now taken hinted at a worry stretching far more than the well-being of the baby – a seed of doubt planted itself uninvited in his head as he began to wonder if the current mental state of his fraa would allow her to go as far as to snatch up someone else's child and then fabricate a story of its unlikely origins. It was a cruel accusation but indeed grief made you do things you did not see yourself capable of and he only wanted to know the truth.

Carefully, he took a few steps forward to his fraa and the boppli secure in her hands, "Please Rebecca, tell me the truth. Where did you find her?" his tone was now demanding but still beseeching to her mercy; craving the honesty of her words.

Rebecca shot him a look as though she had been offended by his latent implication, "I did, James. I went out to lock the barn and I heard a soft whimpering and there she was!" she insisted looking her husband deep in the eyes.

James could see that his fraa was telling him the truth even though the prospect sounded quite bizarre and impossible. But if there was one thing three years of their marriage to each other had given them, it was a sense of trust far stronger than any other bond they could share and so, he resigned to finally believe her, regardless of how unlikely the story sounded.

Rebecca had more thoughts to share, though, as she walked over their bedroom and put the boppli down – she had fallen fast asleep by now and the sight of it made both the Beiler's immobilized in awe.

"I do not know the origins of this child," Rebecca started, "but I do know it was Gott's will for me to find her today. Ach, James! How He works in mysterious ways – my faith was shaken but He restored it ever so swiftly. How wonderful," her voice turned to a soft coo as she once again chained her eyes to the tiny boppli before them.

James gulped loudly, "but we must find her mamm and daed. They must be worried ill!" he exclaimed and then stood down beside the boppli, "how strange and how beautiful."

"I cannot even imagine how someone would voluntarily leave this angel alone in the barn!" Rebecca said, "I shudder to think what would have happened if I had not been there at the right time. Oh how strange indeed."

James pursed his lips and then ran a steady hand over the bundle where the boppli rested in serene slumber. "We must find her parents," he said after a pause.

Rebecca did not reply – for she was contemplating the many thoughts in her head. For a split second, the wicked idea struck her that she would not return this precious bundle of joy – for of course, Gott meant to have her find it and so she should get to keep her. Rebecca found herself lost in the daydream surrounding that idea and imagined this boppli being integrated into the familye that she and James always wanted.

But the thought left her before it could stem its roots in her mind any further. For she realized if she somehow managed to convince James and keep the boppli to herself then she would be doing the same thing that was done to her – snatching away someone's child.

No, that was far too cruel and Rebecca, of all people, realized just how dire the consequences can be after losing a child. Suddenly arching her back upwards and looming over the sleeping boppli protectively, Rebecca arrived to a conclusion.

"You are right – we must find her parents as soon as we possibly can. I will go to any length to return her to her mamm."

--

The next morning the Beiler couple remained true to their earlier promise and dashed into town to find the whereabouts of the boppli's mother. Both Rebecca and James had high hopes that they would be able to find some clue about the whereabouts and origins of the boppli.

One distinct feature about the boppli was that she had brilliant blue eyes that shone with a sparkle and delight for life – this meant that their search for her parents got narrowed down considerably because her eyes were clearly her defining feature and obviously genetically endowed. So holding onto to that lone piece of evidence, Rebecca and James popped on over to the town.

The first person they sought for help Martha Stevens – a local in their community that ran a bread shop.

"Oh how lovely!" she said while seeing them, "what a beautiful boppli. Oh I am so happy for you two – you never even told me you finally gave birth, Rebecca!" the woman complained as she cooed over the baby, arriving at the wrong conclusion.

James shot back a look to Rebecca to see if she was okay – clearly this was still a sensitive topic but Martha simply did not know.

Rebecca swallowed hard and then, by mustering all the will power she could, cracked Martha a small smile. "No, she isn't mine, I am afraid," was she managed to say behind her melancholy smile.

Martha's eyebrows knotted in confusion and then upon seeing the sad grimace that had overtaken the Beiler's, she suddenly clicked together the pieces in her head. "Ach! I am so sorry," she said instantly, "I heard something regarding it – but I thought it was a rumor seeing you here with this boppli today – really, please forgive me."

Rebecca raised up a hand to make her cease her apologies at once, "Please do not. You had no way of knowing."

There was an awkward silence that hung between them for a few moments before James finally spoke up, "the reason we come here today is to ask you about this boppli. It seems that she was thrust into our lives by the most unconventional of ways by Gott," he said.

Martha looked between the two of them in confusion, "what do you mean by this?"

"We found her abandoned in our barn last night without a note or a guardian – we only wish to reunite her with her parents." Rebecca explained in slightly more details.

"Would you be able to tell us who are parents might be?" James added, "or at the very least, give us an idea who might do such a thing?"

Martha was shaking her head all at once, "Nee. Never in my entire life have I seen an event such as this occurring," she said, "how very strange. Lift up the blanket a little and let me have a better look at her."

Martha examined the blue eyed boppli carefully as Rebecca lifted up the veil of her blankets but even that was to no avail as it concluded with Martha shaking her head once again.

"Nee, I do not have a clue," she said to them with an air of finality ringing in her tone.

Rebecca sighed but James shot her a comforting glance, "Do not worry, Rebecca. We still have a lot more people to ask – I am sure someone will be able to aid us. Do not lose hope."

Rebecca nodded and with that they bid Martha adieu and headed on over to continue their search.

The Amish Gift

Also Out Now:

Becoming Amish

Beth Johnson, a young student journalist is sent to join the Amish community to report on their way of life. At first Beth is reluctant to live as they do. But as Beth begins to immerse into the Amish community, she begins to admire their values and strong belief in God. When its time for her to return to her own world, she knows she will miss this way of life, especially Mark Kauffman, someone she has grown very fond of. Beth leaves full of confusion and heartache, she has to make a life-changing decision. Will it be the right one? Will she be accepted and find love and faith in the Amish world? And, can she really become Amish?

Here is a Taster:

State College, Pennsylvania…

"I'm sorry, maybe I didn't hear you right. You want me to live with an Amish family?" Beth Johnson could hear the sarcasm in her voice and strove to keep it under control. She was watching her editor, silently hoping she'd misheard him. She read a little further into the assignment sheet and groaned audibly.

"Beth, just think of the research potential. Sure, we've all heard and seen the Amish, but can you really understand what it's like to live without electricity?" Jack Porter ended his question with an encouraging smile.

Beth looked at him and shook her head, "No, and I'm sure I don't want to. Why can't you assign me to write a story about the Bahamas, or maybe even the Alps. I could do some hands on research there. No problem."

The assignment was for a five-page story about the Amish way of life, written from the perspective of an Englischer, as the Amish referred to anyone non-Amish, who'd experienced their lifestyle firsthand. Firsthand? This was crazy!

Jack laughed, "I bet you could. But, this special edition is about diversity amongst us. Hence, I need an insightful article about the Amish and their way of life. You're the only person who has the time and a flexible schedule this semester. And you have been pestering me to give you something substantial. This is your chance to blow the reader's minds."

Beth sighed, knowing he was right. She was a senior journalism major, and only had a few classes this semester – all of them independent study. That meant she could basically set her own schedule. Jack Porter, the current editor-in-chief of the university newspaper, was her advisor and instructor on record for all of her courses except one.

"When?"

"As soon as you can make the arrangement. I was thinking maybe you could drive up there tomorrow, being as it's Friday, and ask around. Maybe one of the Amish families wouldn't mind having you stay with them for a few days."

"You want me to ask strangers if I can move in with them for a few days?"

"What's the problem? They're Amish. A safer bunch of people you won't find."

"I'm not worried about my safety." At least, not overly so. "It just seems kind of…I don't know, inconsiderate to put people one doesn't know on the spot like that."

Jack smiled at her, "I'm sure you'll manage. Sorry to cut this meeting short, but I have a budget committee meeting in the administration office in three minutes. Do whatever you have to do, but I need that story two weeks from today."

Beth gave him a mock salute as he hurried out of the office. She looked around, just noticing that everyone else had already left to continue their day. "Great! I don't even have anyone to brainstorm with." She groaned again, looking at the assignment sheet with a growing sense of horror. One day without electricity would be torture, but several? There was no way!

She went back to her own workspace and did some thinking about the assignment and how she might convince Jack to give it to someone else. After thirty minutes, she finally had to face the hard facts – her editor was right. She was the only writer in a position to do an assignment like this.

Sighing, she began packing up her computer. She had no idea how she was going to convince an Amish family to let her observe them for a few days, but this was her chance to finally do some real journalism.

Rather than covering another scandal amongst the teaching staff, or writing about how the recipient of this scholarship and that fellowship, she was being given a chance to do something that would require all of her skills. The longer she thought about it, the more she began to think she could actually do this. *Provided I can find a place amongst them.* That was the kicker here. She needed a place to stay and an Amish community that would accept her presence amongst them and not mind answering her questions. And she knew she would have a bunch of those!

She was headed out the door when her cell phone rang, the distinctive tone identifying the caller as her beloved grandfather. "Hey, Grandpa. What's up?"

"Beth, I was hoping I would catch you. I thought maybe you'd like to spend the day with your grandpa tomorrow."

"I'd love to, what are we going to be doing?" she smiled, locking the newspaper office door and heading for her little yellow VW bug.

"Well, I need to make a run down to Lancaster and pick up some furniture pieces I ordered a few weeks back."

"Lancaster? The Amish furniture store?"

"That's the one. Joseph sent word yesterday that everything was ready to be picked up."

Sent word? "So, these people…you know them well?"

"Oh yes. Very nice people. Joseph Kauffman makes some of the finest furniture on the East Coast.

And his wife, Ruth, is a lovely woman. They have six children, I can't remember all of their names, but I believe their oldest is about your age."

Six children? Wow! "I'd love to go up with you. I got a new assignment this morning and maybe you could help me while I help you."

"Darling girl, whatever you need."

"Well, don't say that yet. I'm writing a piece on the Amish lifestyle for a special diversity edition coming out at the end of the semester. My editor thinks I need to spend some quality time amongst the Amish, to get a bird's eye perspective on their lifestyle."

"That's a wonderful idea. Hey! Why don't I speak with Joseph tomorrow and see if you could stay with them for a few days? I bet he wouldn't mind at all."

Beth smiled, once again reminded of how she and her grandfather thought alike. "That would be wonderful. I'd feel much better staying with people someone I trust knows."

"You just leave it to me. Shall I pick you up in the morning?"

"Yes, please."

"I'll see you then. Get a good night's sleep, I plan on putting you to work tomorrow."

"I'll look forward to it. Bye Grandpa."

Lancaster, Pennsylvania…

"Joseph, I'd like to introduce you to my granddaughter, Beth Johnson."

Beth smiled at the man dressed in the black suit, wearing a black hat, and sporting a full face of dark hair. He nodded in her direction, ignoring the hand she extended in greeting. Beth let her hand drop, mentally chiding herself for her lapse. Amish did not touch women they were not related or married to. It wasn't done and being as this wasn't her first time being around them, she should have remembered that.

She'd woken up this morning and dressed in a long brown skirt that ended just above her ankles. She'd paired it with an off-white linen blouse that allowed the light breeze to keep her cool. The intricate stitching around the neckline made her feel feminine, but the serviceable fabric would also allow her to help lift smaller pieces of furniture with ease.

"It's nice to meet you."

"Ja. You are a gut Grossdochder, giving up your time to help."

Beth shared a smile with her grandfather, "Spending time with him is always a good use of my time."

"Beth, I'm going to talk with Joseph for a few minutes. Why don't you take a look around the store?" her grandfather suggested.

"Sure." She smiled at both men and then wandered off, her fingers trailing over the wooden tables and chairs. The furniture wasn't intricately carved, but it was exquisitely finished. The stains used brought to life the texture of the wood, the lights and darks a myriad of beauty.

"Beth?" her grandfather called to her a few moments later.

"Here." She joined them, "Yes?"

"I've spoken to Joseph and he has invited you to spend the week with his family. Isn't that a generous offer?"

A week? Beth hid her dismay and nodded her head, "Yes. Very." A week? I'll be lucky to handle one day without electricity, let alone seven. What have I gotten myself into?

"Thank you very much. Did you mention that I would be writing an article for the school newspaper?"

"I did, and Joseph assured me that he and his family would have no problems answering your questions. He feels that the Englisch truly do not understand why the Amish live like they do. He welcomes any chance to help educate them."

"Mr. Kauffman, I can't thank you enough for trusting me in this matter. I promise I will try to stay out of your way…"

"Nee. In order to fully understand the Amish, one must live like the Amish. That is why you must promise to stay a week."

"When you say live like the Amish, exactly what do you mean?" she asked, afraid she already knew the answer that was forthcoming.

Joseph smiled at her, "You will become one of my dochdern for the week. My wife will teach you what you do not already know, as will my kinner. You must promise to wait until your time amongst us is over before you write your story. "

Beth nodded, "I'll need to take some notes. Will that be a problem?"

"Not at all, but you'll have to write them down on a tablet. We are a conservative Ordnung and there is no electricity in our community."

Great! My worst fears are already coming to fruition. "I understand."

"Gut. You come out Monday morning." Joseph handed her a business card with his address on it.

"You are almost the same size as my Rebecca. You can borrow some of her clothes while you are with us."

"Uhm..okay. Thanks." Now I have to dress like them? This story had better be worth it.

Her grandfather concluded his business a few minutes later and they headed back to the city. "That couldn't have worked out any better," he commented as they left behind the wide open fields and dirt lanes where only black buggies could be seen.

Beth smiled at her grandfather, "This is going to be the longest week of my life."

Her grandfather chuckled, "Chin up, darling. You never know what might happen when you step out of your comfort zone."

Beth nodded, "I'll be sure to let you know how it turns out." This was going to be way beyond anything resembling her comfort zone. But she was journalist and she would persevere. Jack had often told his reporters that being a journalist was hard work and required sacrifice at times. Learning how to succeed in difficult circumstances set good journalists apart from great journalists. Beth wanted to be the latter, so this assignment would be good practice for her future career. She just needed to stay focused on the end game. Write a fabulous piece!

Becoming Amish

Made in the USA
Coppell, TX
02 March 2022

74354475R00049